PROJECT

M000099188

Sound and Light

Terry Jennings

Illustrated by **David Anstey**

CONTENTS

SMITHMARK

SOUNDS

Every day we hear hundreds of sounds. These can be loud or soft, high or low sounds. Listen carefully. How many sounds can you hear?

Look at the picture. Have you heard any of these? What type of sounds are they? All sounds are different, but they are all made in the same way. A sound is made when something moves back and forth quickly, or *vibrates*.

A drum vibrates when it is hit. If we hit it harder the sound gets louder. We hear normal sound with our ears.

4

TEST YOUR HEARING

When somewhere is really quiet we say it is so quiet we can hear a pin drop. Can you hear a pin drop? Work with a friend in a quiet room.

1 Stand a ruler up in modeling clay on the table.

2 Stand in front of the table with your back to it. Ask your friend to drop the pin from the top of the ruler. Can you hear it?

3 Keep moving further and further away until you can no longer hear it.

Change places with your friend. Which of you has the better hearing? Drop a coin instead of a pin. What differences do you find?

Test your family. Who is best at hearing soft sounds?

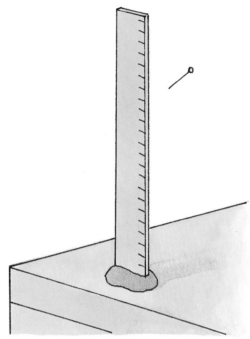

ARE TWO EARS BETTER THAN ONE?

Blindfold a friend with a scarf. Ask your friend to cover one ear. Tap two coins together and ask your friend to point to the sound.

Now do it again and ask your friend to listen with two ears. Are two ears better?

Play a sound guessing game. Blindfold your friend with a scarf. Make different sounds and ask your friend to listen with one ear. Can he or she guess what is making the sounds? Now ask your friend to listen with both ears. Are two ears better for this?

Change places with your friend. Can you do better?

HOW SOUND TRAVELS

When things vibrate by being banged or tapped, they make a sound. Sounds from the vibrating objects travel through the air to reach our ears. Without air we could not hear most sounds. Sounds travel in waves. When these spread out in the air, everyone can hear them.

Sometimes sounds may be lost in general noise. We can channel these sound waves to make them easier to hear. One way to channel the sound waves our voices make is by speaking into a tube. That way the sounds do not get lost.

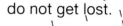

MAKE A SPEAKING TUBE

On ships, sailors used to use a speaking tube. Then the sailors on the deck of the ship could speak to the captain in bed below. Make your own speaking tube and see how it works.

1 Push one funnel in each end of the hose.

2 Take one end of the speaking tube upstairs. Speak into the funnel while your friend puts the other funnel against his or her ear. Can your friend downstairs hear you?

You will need: a length of clean hose; 2 clean funnels.

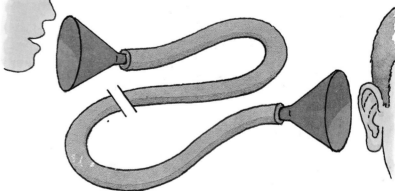

HOW DO EARS WORK?

We hear sounds because we have ears. If you look at the picture you can see how the ear works.

When our brain gets the sound message, it tells us what the ear-drums hear.

You can see for yourself how your ear-drums work if you do this simple experiment.

Turn a radio or television on so that it is making a loud sound. Hold a sheet of thin paper in front of the loudspeaker. Can you feel and see the paper vibrating? This is the way our ear-drums vibrate when we hear sounds.

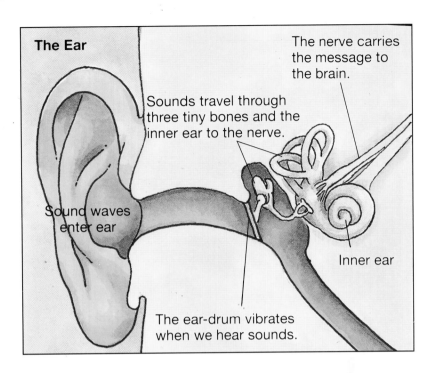

The Ear

The nerve carries the message to the brain.

Sounds travel through three tiny bones and the inner ear to the nerve.

Sound waves enter ear

Inner ear

The ear-drum vibrates when we hear sounds.

IMPROVE YOUR HEARING

Many years ago people used ear trumpets to help them hear better. Make one for yourself and see if it helps you to hear.

1 Roll up a large sheet of paper.

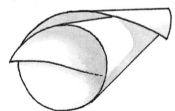

2 Tape down the edges. Cut the tip off.

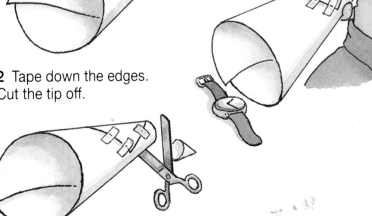

3 Put the ear trumpet to your ear. Listen to a soft sound such as the ticking of a watch or small clock. Can you hear better with your ear trumpet?

Helpful Ears

Some animals have large ears which help them to hear soft sounds. Foxes, rabbits, and deer have large ears. Foxes need to be able to hear the animals they are hunting. Rabbits and deer need to be able to hear their enemies.

Some people cannot hear very well at all. They are deaf. Deaf people wear hearing aids to help them hear better.

SOUND MESSAGES

We have seen that sounds travel through the air. What else will they go through? Will sounds go along a piece of string? Make this fun *telephone*, for three people, to find out.

MAKE A TELEPHONE

You will need: 3 clean round, pint-size ice cream cups; 2 long pieces of string; 3 toothpicks.

1 Ask an adult to make a small hole in the bottom of each container.

2 Take one piece of the string and thread it through the holes in two of the cups. Tie each end to a toothpick.

3 Tie the second piece of string to the middle of the first.

4 Fix the third cup in the same way as the other two.

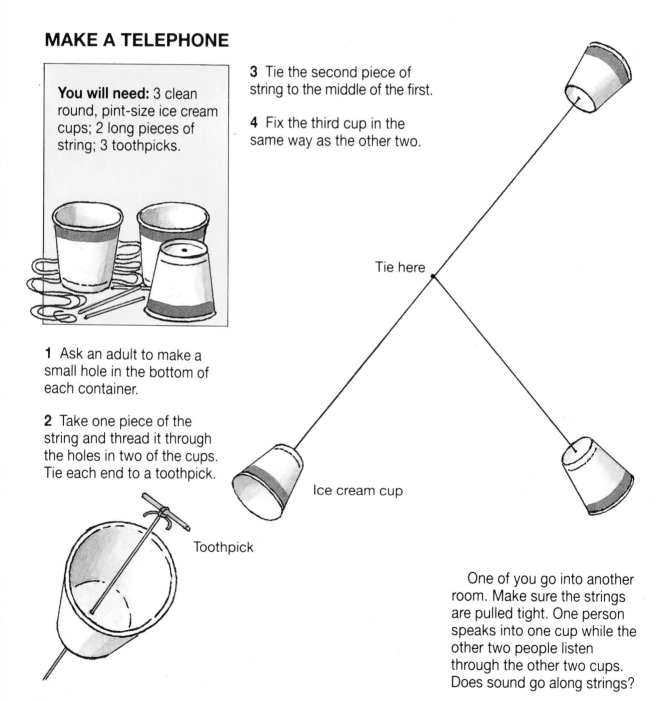

Tie here

Ice cream cup

Toothpick

One of you go into another room. Make sure the strings are pulled tight. One person speaks into one cup while the other two people listen through the other two cups. Does sound go along strings?

8

LISTENING IN

Sound travels through many kinds of material. Test which objects carry sound best.

Have you seen pictures of hunters with their ears to the ground? Why do you think they do this? Pretend to be a hunter and track a friend.

Make sure your friend is out of sight, but moving. Put your ear to the floor and listen. Can you hear footsteps more clearly? Do sounds travel better through the floor than they do through the air? Track them on grass and on carpet. What do you notice?

Secret Messages

People in prison sometimes send messages along pipes. It may just be a tapping sound to let one prisoner know that another is close by. Or, it could be a secret message in code.

Can you hear sounds through cold water pipes from one room to the next? You could make up your own code.

NEVER touch hot water pipes. They can burn.

Do sounds travel through water? Blow up a balloon. Hold it against one ear. Press a ticking watch against the balloon. Can you hear the watch ticking through the air in the balloon? Now fill the balloon with water and tie the top. Can you still hear the watch ticking through the water in the balloon?

What everyday objects do we use to give out sounds? Look at the pictures for clues.

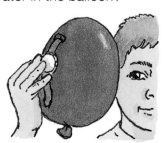

THE HUMAN VOICE

We use our voice to speak. When we speak our *voice-box* vibrates to make the sounds. Look at the picture below. Put your fingers over your voice-box as you talk. Can you feel the vibrations?

Collect some large containers such as buckets and boxes. Talk into them. How does your voice change? Can you guess what is happening to the sound? You can make your voice even louder and clearer with a megaphone.

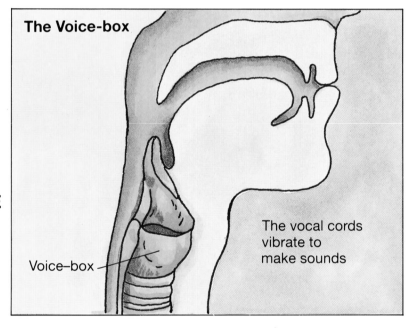

The Voice-box

The vocal cords vibrate to make sounds

Voice–box

MAKE A MEGAPHONE

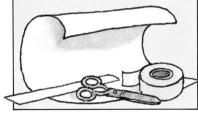

You will need: a piece of stiff cardboard; roll of thin poster board; tape; scissors.

1 Roll a sheet of poster board into a cone.

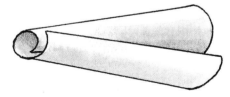

2 Fix the ends with tape. Cut off the point of the cone.

3 Cut out a strip of cardboard and bend both ends, to make a handle. Fix the handle to your megaphone with tape.

Ask a friend to stand a long way away from you. Shout a message. Can your friend hear you clearly? Now shout the message through your megaphone. Is it clearer now?

Make a list of people who sometimes use megaphones. When do they use them?

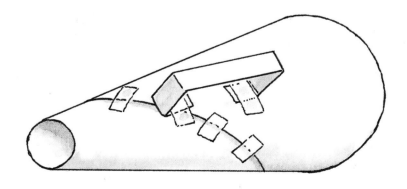

KEEPING OUT SOUNDS

We call sounds we do not like, noise. What sounds do you not like? How can we keep out sounds?

1 Take a small radio. Turn the sound on loud. Put the radio in a large cardboard box, with a lid. Can you still hear the sound?

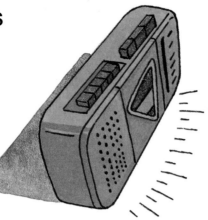

2 Wad up some newspaper. Pack it around the radio. Does it make a difference?

Try other materials around the radio. Which is best at keeping out sounds? Make a chart of what you find.

MAKE EAR MUFFS

You will need: a plastic hair band; foam rubber or sponge; double-sided tape; scissors.

1 Cut out two circles of foam rubber or sponge.

2 Stick a piece of tape on both ends of the hair band.

3 Attach your sponge circles to the tape.

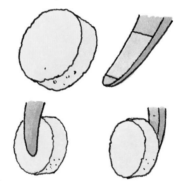

Do ear muffs stop sounds?

Try two circles of sponge on each side of your hair band to make your ear muffs thicker. Do they stop more sounds?

Try other materials such as cotton, paper, felt, and plastic bubble packing. Which material is best at stopping sound? Make a chart and compare it with your first chart. Are they the same?

Loud Sounds

Loud sounds can damage your ears. They could make you deaf. This man wears ear protectors to keep his ears from being damaged.

We shouldn't always keep out loud sounds. They can act as a warning of danger. This boy is listening to very loud music. There are two dangers, what do you think they are?

MAKING SOUNDS

We have seen that when an object vibrates it makes a sound. This fact can be used to make many different kinds of *musical instruments*.

MAKE A DRUM

Collect tins of different sizes. Stand them in a row. Hit each of them with a stick. Do they all make the same sound?

1 Take a large tin. Cover the open end with thin plastic or plastic wrap to make a drum. Pull it as tight as you can. Hold it in place with a rubber band or string like this.

2 Sprinkle a little rice on top of the drum and gently beat it with a teaspoon. Watch what happens to the rice. Why does this happen?

MAKE A XYLOPHONE

A xylophone is another instrument that you hit to make sounds. These sounds are like a series of bells. Make your own xylophone and try to play a tune on it.

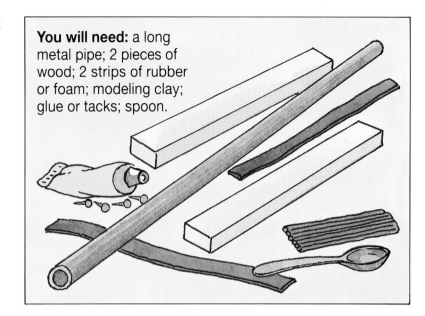

You will need: a long metal pipe; 2 pieces of wood; 2 strips of rubber or foam; modeling clay; glue or tacks; spoon.

1 Ask an adult to cut the pipe into different lengths.

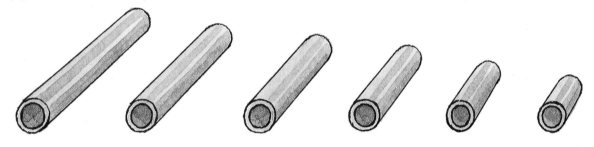

2 Lay two strips of wood on the table and glue or tack the rubber or foam to them.

3 Arrange the metal tubes on top as shown, using modeling clay to keep them in place.

Tap the tubes with a spoon. Which tube makes the highest sound? Tap one of the tubes again. Now lightly touch it with your fingers. Can you feel the metal vibrating? What happens if you press your fingers down on one of the tubes after you have hit it?

Instead of metal tubes you could try different lengths of wood or plastic.

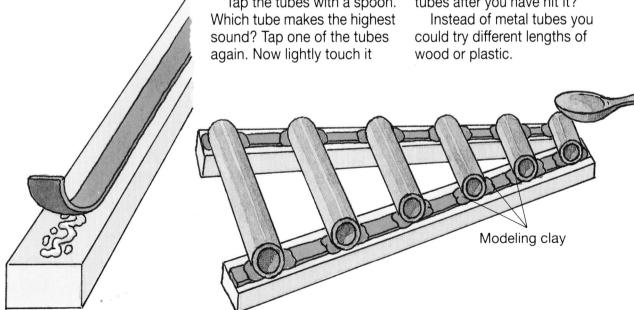

Modeling clay

SHAKE AND BLOW

Sounds can also be produced when objects are shaken or when air is blown over things with holes in them. Have you ever shaken a box or tin to see what is in it? Have you ever heard the wind whistling through the trees or down the chimney?

WIND INSTRUMENTS

> **You will need:** 5 glass bottles, all the same shape and size; water.

2 Put a little clean water in the next one, a little more in the next, and so on.

3 Almost fill the last bottle.

1 Put your bottles in a line. Leave one bottle empty.

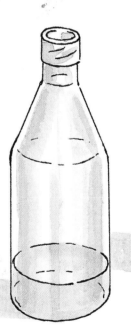

Blow across the top of each bottle in turn.
Which one makes the highest sound? There is a different amount of air in each bottle. Does it change the sound?

Use a teaspoon or pencil to tap your bottles. Listen to the sound they make. What do you notice? Which bottle makes a high sound? Which bottle makes a low sound? Are the sounds the same as when you blow across the bottles? Can you play a tune on your bottles?

MAKE MARACAS

Some musical instruments are shaken instead of being hit. Maracas are instruments that are shaken.

You will need: 2 clean plastic bottles; a stick; strong sticky parcel tape; small stones.

1 Remove the top from one of the bottles.

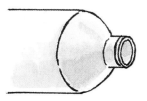

2 Make sure the stick fits tightly in the neck.

3 Cut the stick into two.

4 Drop the stones in.

5 Push the stick hard into the top to make a handle.

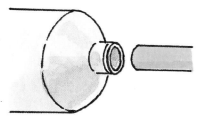

Follow the instructions to make your second maracas. They are shaken in pairs. You could decorate them with stickers or paints.

Make other maracas from cardboard, metal, and plastic containers. Put different materials inside. You could try beads, dried peas, beans, and other seeds. Do the sounds they make change if you use different containers and different materials to go inside them?

Use your maracas to accompany music.

6 Wrap the tape tightly around the top of the bottle and the stick.

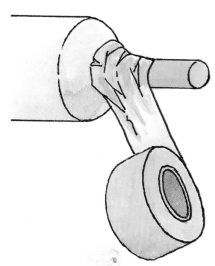

MUSICAL SOUNDS

In the last project you saw that you could make sounds by blowing across the top of a bottle. You can also make sounds by blowing through a tube and plucking strings.

MAKE A STRAW PIPE

You will need: plastic drinking straws; a pair of round-ended scissors.

1 Flatten one end of a straw for about 1 inch (2 or 3 cm)

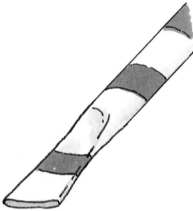

2 Cut off the corners. Blow down the straw. Can you make a note? You may need to practice.

3 Cut off a small piece of the straw at the other end and blow again. Is the note higher or lower?

4 Make several straw pipes of different lengths. Can you play a tune? What happens if you blow into two or three straws at the same time? You could tape the pipes together to make Pan pipes.

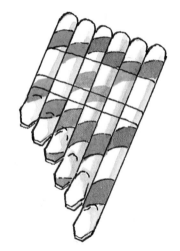

Twanging Sounds

We have already seen a number of objects that vibrate and make sounds. You can use other things that vibrate to make different sounds.

1 Hold one end of a plastic ruler firmly over the edge of a table.

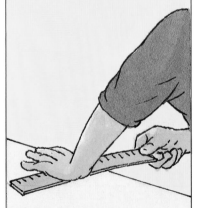

2 Twang the other end. What happens?

3 Change the length of ruler sticking out.

4 Twang it again. Does it make the same sound?

Strings will also vibrate if they are twanged, or plucked. This is how a guitar works.

MAKE A GUITAR

You will need: a rigid plastic rectangular box; long piece of wood; 12 small screws and a screwdriver; 4 lengths of nylon twine or fine string. Ask an adult to help you.

1 Screw the wood onto the bottom of the box.

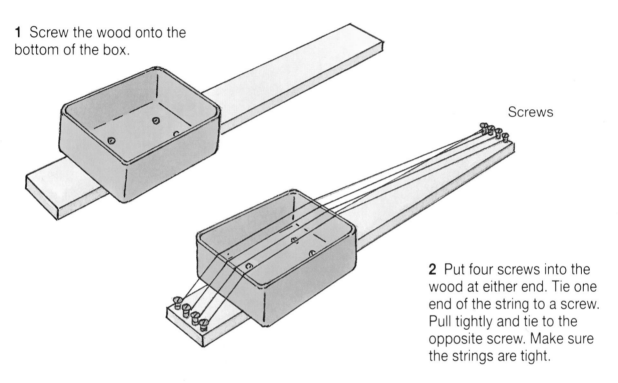

Screws

2 Put four screws into the wood at either end. Tie one end of the string to a screw. Pull tightly and tie to the opposite screw. Make sure the strings are tight.

MAKE AN ORCHESTRA

Now you and your friends can use all the instruments you have made to make an *orchestra*.

An orchestra has three main types of instruments; stringed, wind, and *percussion*. Have you got all three kinds? You will need a conductor. What does a conductor do?

Now you can all try to play a well-known tune.

17

LIGHT

We have seen that sound travels in waves. Light also travels in waves. Look at the picture. Light enables us to see the things around us.

Long ago people only had the light of the sun to see by and they worked only in the daytime. Nowadays we have electric lights to let us see and work at night. We can see things only when the light is shining on them. We cannot see without light. We see things with our eyes.

WHERE DOES LIGHT COME FROM?

Make a collection of candles.
1 Stand one up in a dish of sand. Ask an adult to light the candle for you. Look at the flame. What color is it?

NEVER play with matches or candles, or touch hot light bulbs.

2 Blow out the candle. Light another one and look at the flame. Make a chart to show in what ways the flames differ and in what ways they are the same. Does it matter what color the wax is?

3 Look at the flame of the candle carefully. Now draw the curtains. How does the flame look different? Is the flame really different?

Make a collection of flashlights with your friends. Look at them carefully. In what ways are they all alike? How are they different? What materials are the flashlights made of? How is the light they give different?

The sun gives us heat as well as light. Do all lights give out heat?

DOES LIGHT GO AROUND CORNERS?

Does light travel in straight lines or will it go around corners? You can find out below.

You will need: 3 pieces of cardboard; black paper; flashlight; knitting needle; modeling clay; pencil; ruler.

1 To find the middles of the pieces of cardboard, draw lines across each piece.

2 Use the pencil to make a neat hole in the middle of each piece.

3 Hold one of the pieces of cardboard at arm's length. What do you see? Now move it slowly toward your eye. What happens?

4 Stand all three in a row, using modeling clay to keep them upright.

5 Push a knitting needle through the holes to make sure they are in a straight line.

6 Hold a piece of black paper behind one.

7 Shine a flashlight through the holes. Where does the spot of light fall?

8 Move the black paper and shine the flashlight from the other end of the row. Where does the spot of light fall?

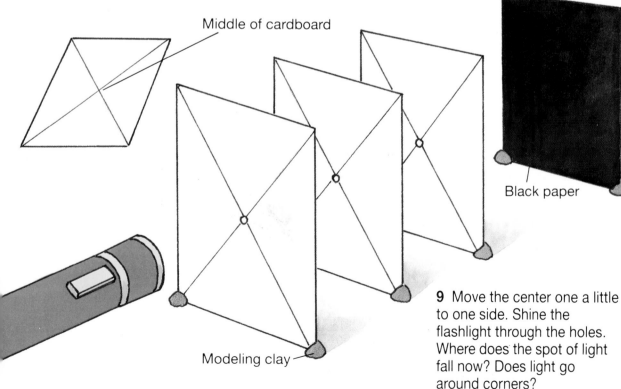

Middle of cardboard

Black paper

Modeling clay

9 Move the center one a little to one side. Shine the flashlight through the holes. Where does the spot of light fall now? Does light go around corners?

HOW LIGHT BEHAVES

We are used to seeing through glass windows. We can see through windows because light can go through the glass in them. But we cannot see through all materials.

Things that we can see through clearly, like the glass of a window, are said to be *transparent*. Things that let some light through, but not enough to see clearly, are *translucent*. Things that do not let any light through are *opaque*.

WHAT CAN LIGHT PASS THROUGH?

Make a collection of everyday containers. Collect tins, bags, bottles, and jars.

1 Set up a flashlight or a desk lamp so that the light shines toward you.

2 Hold each of the things up to the light. How much light can you see?

Make a chart showing how much light you can see through all your objects.

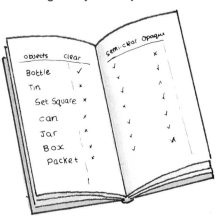

Shadows

Shadows are made when light cannot pass through an object. Look at some shadows outside. Watch what happens to a shadow during a sunny day.

MAKE A SHADOW CLOCK

You will need: a light colored box; stick; pencil; tape.

1 Attach the stick to the box with tape.

2 Put the box in a sunny place.

3 Mark on the box where the shadow falls. Write down the time, next to your mark.

4 Do this at least five times during the day.

5 Finally see what time the longest shadow from the stick is.

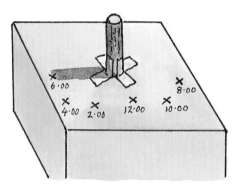

You can use your shadow clock box to tell the time. As long as it is sunny and you always place the box in the same place, you can check the time.

CAN LIGHT BEND?

You have seen that light cannot travel around corners. You have also seen that it will not travel through opaque substances. Can it bend?

This next experiment will surprise your friends.

You will need: a stone; dish; water.

1 Place the stone in the dish.

2 Ask your friends to move slowly away from the table until they can no longer see the stone.

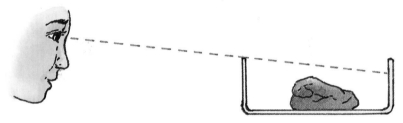

3 Pour water into the dish. They will be very surprised.

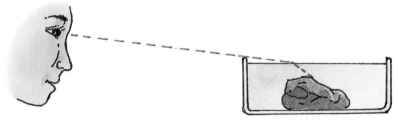

When light passes from air into water it slows down and changes direction or is

Tell them you will move the stone, without touching it, so that they can see it again.

refracted. This makes objects appear to be in a different place.

PROJECT SCIENCE

MIRROR IMAGES

A lot of the light that falls on things "bounces off" again. We say it is *reflected*. If the surface is rough, like a brick or a newspaper, the light is scattered in all directions. If the surface is smooth and shiny, it makes a *mirror*. In a mirror we can see images or reflections of things held in front of it.

USING MIRRORS

Make a collection of shiny things. You could use pots, pans, ornaments, mirrors, knives, coins, aluminum foil, and Christmas decorations.

Where are the shiny places, or highlights, on them?

Can you see your face in any of them? What does it look like? Does it look the same in each object? Can you guess how it will look in each one?

Look in a real mirror. Touch your left ear. Which ear does your reflection seem to touch?

MAGIC WRITING

Look at the picture. Can you read what it says? It is a secret message. Look at it in the reflection of a mirror. Can you read it now? Write a short message on a piece of paper. Look at the message in a mirror. Copy it out as it looks in the mirror, and give it to a friend. Can your friend read the message? Ask them to write one for you.

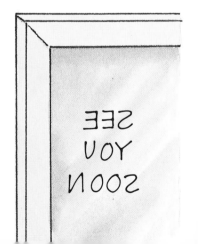

We use mirrors a lot in everyday life, and not just to see what we look like. Cars have mirrors so that drivers can see behind them.

Dentists use small mirrors so that they can see all parts of your teeth.

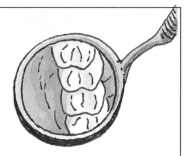

MAKE A PERISCOPE

You will need: a cube of wood; 2 small mirrors; 2 strips of wood; hammer; nails; glue.

1 Ask an adult to help you saw the cube of wood in half.

2 Nail the two halves onto the two strips of wood.

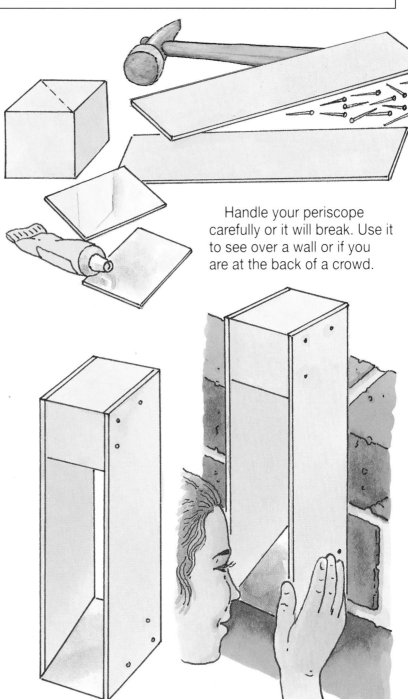

Handle your periscope carefully or it will break. Use it to see over a wall or if you are at the back of a crowd.

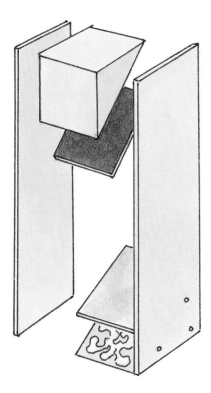

3 Glue the mirrors onto the two halves of wood.

COLORS

On a sunny day we can see a blue sky and green trees. We see sunlight as only one color. Is it really just one color? You can find out in this next experiment.

MAKE A RAINBOW

You will need: a shallow dish of water; mirror; oil; sheet of black paper.

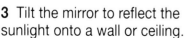

The band of colors that you can see reflected is called a spectrum. Name all the colors.

A rainbow is a spectrum in the sky. Rainbows appear when it rains while the sun is shining. The drops of rain break up the sunlight into the colors of the rainbow.

1 Place the dish on a sunny windowsill.

2 Put a mirror in the water.

3 Tilt the mirror to reflect the sunlight onto a wall or ceiling.

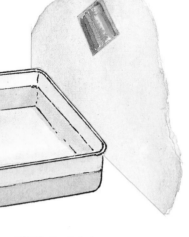

MIXING COLORS

1 Mix red and yellow paints. What happens? Try mixing other colors. Make your own chart to show what happens.

2 Look at the chart in the picture. Is yours the same?

4 Slide the piece of black paper under the dish.

5 Put two or three drops of oil on the water. What happens?

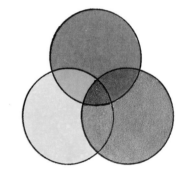

24

MORE LIGHT COLORS

You will need: cardboard; red and yellow paints or pens; pencil.

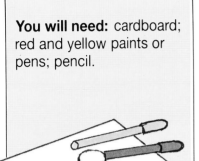

1 Use the lid of a jar to draw a circle. Cut it out and divide it into four quarters.

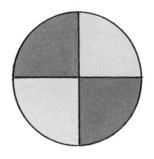

2 Color two of the quarters red and yellow. Make a small hole in the center.

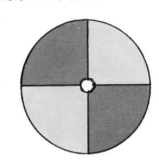

3 Push your pencil through it to make a spinning top. Spin your top. What color does it seem to be? Try using other colors.

COLORED LIGHTS

You will need: red, blue, and green cellophane; 3 flashlights; cardboard; scissors; tape; white paper.

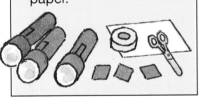

1 Cut out three pieces of cardboard to fit the flashlights.

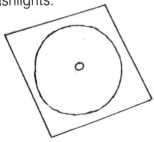

2 Make a hole in the center of each one.

3 Fix a different colored piece of cellophane over each mask hole.

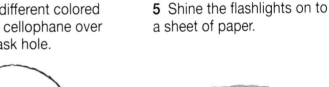

4 Fix the masks to the flashlights.

Tape

Mask

5 Shine the flashlights on to a sheet of paper.

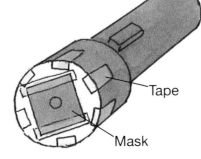

What color do you see on the paper? Try mixing other colored lights. Do colored lights mix in the same way as colored paints?

25

IN FOCUS

A *magnifying glass* is a piece of curved glass. It bends the rays of light as they pass through it. Then things look bigger.

You can see how a magnifying glass bends the sun's rays into a very small spot. On a sunny day, hold a magnifying glass above a sheet of scrap paper. Move the magnifying glass up and down a little until you see a bright spot of light on the paper. It is now in *focus*. Hold the magnifying glass still. Look for wisps of smoke as the sun's rays begin to heat the paper. REMOVE THE PAPER IMMEDIATELY.

NEVER set fire to anything.

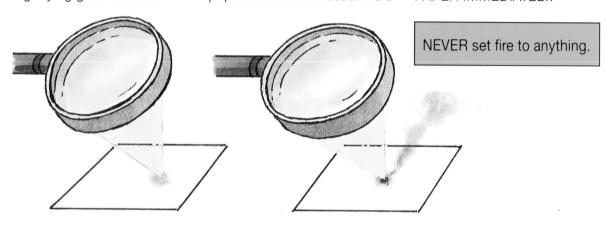

MAKE A SIMPLE MAGNIFYING GLASS

Put your finger into a jar of water. Why does your finger seem bigger? Is it because of the water? Is it because of the shape of the glass?

Find a clear plastic lid. Coffee cans sometimes have suitable ones. Make a small hole in the lid with a pin.

Cover the hole with one drop of water. Look through the hole at some writing. Does the writing look bigger? You have made a magnifying glass.

Use a real magnifying glass to look at small plants and animals. Does it make things look twice as big, or more?

Make a collection of things that magnify. The part you see through is called the *lens*. Feel the lenses gently. What shape are they? Are lenses always transparent?

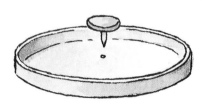

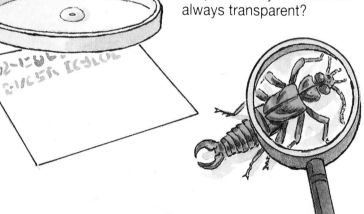

MAKE A SIMPLE TELESCOPE

You will need: 2 lenses (one should magnify larger than the other); short piece of wood; modeling clay.

You may be able to get some lenses from old *eyeglasses*.

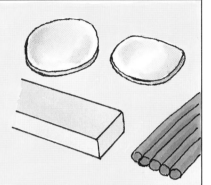

NEVER look at the sun through a lens. It could damage your eyes.

Lenses

We use lenses in lots of everyday things. Some of them are shown in the pictures below. They are all used in different ways. What are they used for?

1 Ask an adult to cut some grooves across the piece of wood for you.

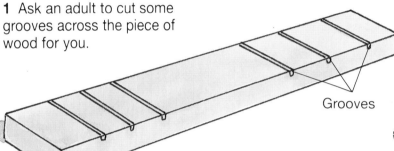

Grooves

2 Stand two lenses in two of the grooves. Hold them in place with modeling clay.

Modeling clay

Lens

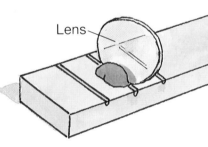

3 Look through the two lenses together.

Can you make things look bigger or smaller with your telescope? Can you see a sharp picture through the lenses? Do some things seem upside down?

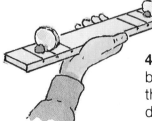

4 Change the distance between the lenses and look through them again. What differences do you see?

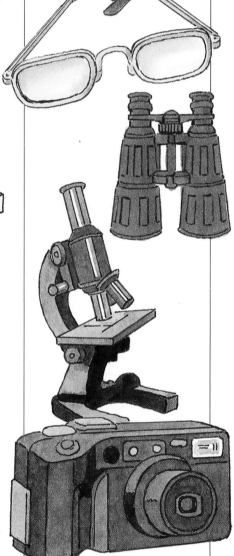

HOW YOU SEE

We see with our eyes. We see only a small part of each eye when we look in a mirror. Each eye is shaped like a ball. The important parts of the eye are shown here.

● The *cornea* is transparent and lets light into the eye. The light goes through a hole in the centre of the eye called the *pupil*.

● The *lens* changes shape. This means we can see objects near and far away. A picture of the object forms on the *retina*.

● The nerve sends a message about the picture to the brain. The brain then tells us what we are looking at.

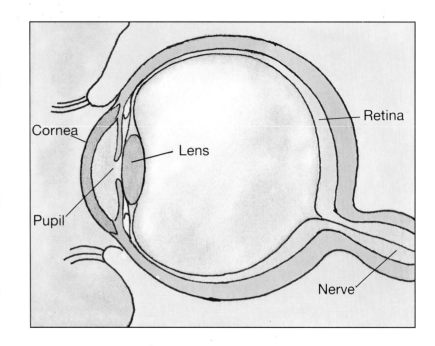

ARE TWO EYES BETTER THAN ONE?

Hold one finger out in front of you. Close one eye. Bring your other hand around quickly and try to touch the two fingers together. Can you do it?

   Now try again with both eyes open. Is it easier or more difficult?

1 Stand a ruler up in modeling clay.

2 Close one eye and put a finger in front of it. Make sure it is exactly in line.

3 Open your eye and close the other one. Is your finger still in line?

   Now try with both eyes open. Which is easier?

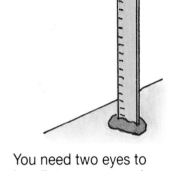

You need two eyes to judge distances properly and to see that things have depth. Walk around the room with one eye closed. What differences do you notice?

IS SEEING BELIEVING?

Sometimes our eyes trick us. What we think we see is not true. We call this effect an *optical illusion*.

Look at these pictures. Which of the straight lines is longest? Now measure them.

Look at this picture quickly. What do you see? Do you see a young girl or an old woman?

Is the hat taller than it is wide? Measure it and see.

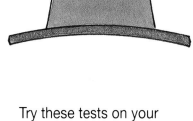

Try these tests on your friends. Do they see the same as you?

Draw a fish on one side of a piece of cardboard. Draw a bowl on the other. Put the cardboard in the split end of a piece of cane. Spin it. What happens?

Which of the central orange circles is largest? Now measure them. Were you right?

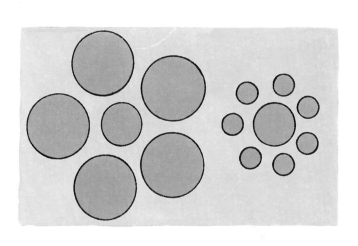

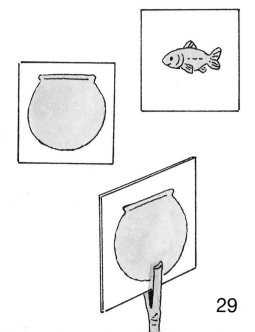

USING LIGHT

The animals we see in the daytime – such as butterflies and birds – like the light. Some animals prefer the dark. Many moths only come out at night. So do most owls, foxes, and mice.

What about the small animals you find in the soil and under stones and wood? Do they prefer the light or the dark? You can test this in the following experiment.

MAKE A CHOICE CHAMBER

You will need: some sow bugs; shoe box; black paper; plastic wrap; jar; plastic spoon; cloth; pencil.

1 Look under large stones and rotting logs for sow bugs.

2 Collect a few in a jar with rotting leaves for food. Don't pick them up with your fingers, use a plastic spoon. Be sure to put the stones or logs back exactly as you found them.

3 Cover the jar with a piece of cloth to keep the sow bugs safe.

4 Draw a line across the middle of your box.

5 Cut a small hole in one side of the box and plug it up with wadded up paper.

6 Cover one half of the box with plastic wrap and the other half with black paper.

7 Carefully put your sow bugs in the box through the hole in the side.

8 Plug the hole again.

Leave the sow bugs for 10 minutes. Then look to see where they are now. Are they in the dark part of the box or the light part?

Now try the experiment with some small earthworms, slugs, or snails. Do they prefer the light or the dark? When you have found out, put all the small animals back where you found them.

STAYING HIDDEN

Some animals use patterns of color or light and dark to stay hidden from their enemies. We say they are *camouflaged*. In this picture there are six creatures hiding. Read the list and see how many you can find.

Look for a: bird; eggs; lizard; grasshopper; stick insect; caterpillar.

Hunt the Moth

You can make your own camouflaged insects and play a game with friends.

1 Cut out several moth shapes.

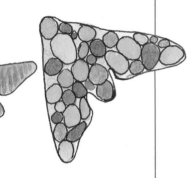

2 Color them to hide in different places. See how many your friends find.

People camouflage themselves too. Look at the pictures. Why do these people need to hide?

Birdwatcher

Soldier

Can you camouflage yourself so that you can hide from your friends? Play a game of camouflage hide-and-seek.

PLANTS AND LIGHT

Plants need light to grow and make their food. See how many plants you can name. Grasses are plants. Without light they would die.

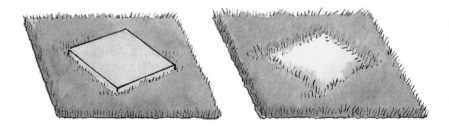

You can test this for yourself by this small experiment.

1 Cover a small patch of grass for a few days.

2 Take away your cover. What has happened to the grass in the second picture?

Leave the grass uncovered. What happens?

MAKE A CIRCULAR BEAN

Do you think it's possible to make a bean grow in a circle? Why don't you try?

You will need: a large cardboard box; plant pot; soil or compost; runner bean seed.

1 Plant your seed in the flowerpot of soil. Make sure you keep it well watered.

2 When the shoot is about 6 inches (15 cm) high, it is ready to use.

3 Cut a hole in the box. Put the box over the plant making sure the hole faces a window.

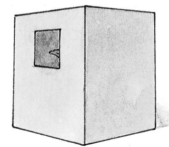

4 After two or three days carefully lift the box. The bean will have grown toward the light coming in the hole.

Turn the plant a few inches in one direction. Put the box back.

Do this every two days. Eventually your bean plant will have grown in a complete circle.

MAKE A BEAN PLANT MAZE

You will need: a small runner bean plant; a long narrow box with a lid.

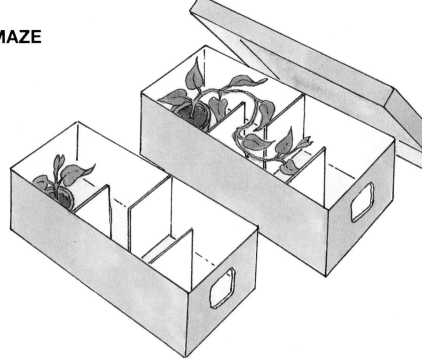

1 Cut a small hole in one end of the box.

2 Make cardboard partitions.

3 Stand the bean plant at the back. Put the lid on the box and leave the plant for a few days.

4 Lift the lid off the box carefully. Has your bean found its way through your maze to the light?

GROW YOUR INITIALS

You will need: a piece of flannel; dish; alfalfa seeds.

1 Wet the flannel and lay it on a saucer or dish.

Sprinkle the flannel with alfalfa seeds in the shape of your initials.

2 Stand the saucer on a sunny windowsill. Do not let the flannel dry out.

3 Plant another piece of flannel in the same way. Put the saucer in a dark closet.

Do both sets of your initials grow? How are they different?

Hairy Eggmen

Another idea is to paint faces on clean eggshells.

1 Fill your eggshells with moist cotton.

2 Grow alfalfa seeds or grass seeds on the cotton so that it looks like hair growing on your egg people's heads.

GLOSSARY

Here are the meanings of some words you might have met for the first time in this book.

CAMOUFLAGE: an animal whose color matches its surroundings so making it hard to see is said to be camouflaged.

CORNEA: a thin transparent skin that covers the front of the eye.

EYEGLASSES: a pair of lenses in a frame to help a person see more clearly.

LENS: a piece of glass or plastic with a slightly curved surface. Some lenses magnify or make things look bigger, others make things look smaller.

MAGNIFYING GLASS: a lens or group of lenses that make objects look larger.

MIRROR: a glass or metal surface that reflects things clearly.

MUSICAL INSTRUMENT: something that makes music.

OPAQUE: not letting light through.

OPTICAL ILLUSION: something we see but which is not really as it seems.

ORCHESTRA: a large number of musicians who play together.

PERCUSSION INSTRUMENT: a musical instrument played by hitting or shaking.

PUPIL: the round opening in the middle of the eye.

REFLECT: to throw back or turn back light. To show an image or "picture" in a mirror.

REFRACT: to bend or change the direction of light.

RETINA: the lining at the back of the eye which is sensitive to light.

SHADOWS: the dark shapes that appear on the ground, on a wall or on some other screen when objects are between it and the light.

SPECTRUM: a rainbow-colored band of light seen when white light is split up into the colors it is made of.

TELEPHONE: a device that lets us speak to someone a long way away.

TRANSLUCENT: letting some light through but not enough to see through.

TRANSPARENT: letting light through so that it is clear enough to see through.

VIBRATE: moving rapidly back and forth.

VOICE-BOX: the lump in the neck, sometimes called the Adam's apple, which helps us to speak.